Chocol Making for Beginners

Beginner's Guide to Techniques and Tools Needed to Make Delicious Homemade Chocolate Which You Can Enjoy Yourself, Use as Gifts or Sell to Make Some Extra Cash

By Luke Rosado

© **Copyright 2020 - All rights reserved.**

The content contained within this book may not be reproduced, duplicated or transmitted without direct written permission from the author or the publisher.

Under no circumstances will any blame or legal responsibility be held against the publisher or author for any damages, reparation, or monetary loss due to the information contained within this book. Either directly or indirectly.

Legal Notice:

This book is copyright protected. This book is only for personal use. You cannot amend, distribute, sell, use, quote or paraphrase any part, or the content within this book, without the consent of the author or publisher.

Disclaimer Notice:

Please note the information contained within this document is for educational and entertainment purposes only. All effort has been executed to present accurate, up to date and reliable, complete information. No warranties of any kind are declared or implied. Readers acknowledge that the author is not engaging in the rendering of legal, financial, medical or professional advice. The content within this book has been derived from various sources. Please consult a licensed professional before attempting any techniques outlined in this book.

By reading this document, the reader agrees that under no circumstances is the author responsible for any losses, direct or indirect, which are incurred as a result of the use of information contained within this document, including, but not limited to, —errors, omissions, or inaccuracies.

Contents

Chapter 1—Reasons for Making Homemade Chocolate? 1

Chapter 2—How Chocolate is Usually Made 4

Chapter 3-- Making Terrific Homemade Chocolate Easily 7

Chapter 4-- Finest Kinds Of Chocolate to Utilize in Homemade Chocolate 10

Chapter 5-- Tools for Creating Homemade Chocolate 14

Chapter 6—How to Make Sugar Free Chocolate 17

Chapter 7—How to Make Low Fat Chocolate 21

Chapter 8—How to Make Your Chocolate Distinct 24

Chapter 9-- Molds 27

Chapter 10—How to Make a Better Homemade Chocolate 30

Chapter 11—How to Wrap Your Homemade Chocolate 34

Chapter 12-- Homemade Chocolate Christmas Ideas............................37

Chapter 13-- Homemade Chocolate Drinks for Holidays.......................40

Chapter 14-- Homemade Chocolate Easter Ideas..................................44

Chapter 15-- Homemade Chocolate Ideas for Other Holidays 47

    For Valentine's Day..47

    For Mother's Day 50

Chapter 16-- Homemade Chocolate Birthdays Ideas 53

Chapter 17-- Homemade Chocolate Ideas for Weddings and Wedding Showers 57

    Homemade Chocolate Ideas for Wedding Showers 59

Chapter 18-- Homemade Chocolate Ideas for Other Celebrations.........63

Chapter 19-- Gourmet Homemade Chocolate.......................................66

Chapter 20-- Selling Homemade Chocolate and Making Money............70

Conclusion 74

Thank you for buying this book and I hope that you will find it useful. If you will want to share your thoughts on this book, you can do so by leaving a review on the Amazon page, it helps me out a lot.

Chapter 1—Reasons for Making Homemade Chocolate?

Many people have never ever truly even though about making their own homemade chocolate, they simply purchase chocolate bars or chocolate cookies at the shop and do not hesitate about it. However, individuals have actually been making homemade chocolate for centuries. Some individuals believe that homemade chocolate tastes better than retail chocolate. And who does not like getting a special chocolate reward that was created just for them?

For individuals that have unique medical conditions or dietary obstacles that make it unhealthy for them to consume commercial chocolate that is filled with sugar and fat making homemade chocolate is an excellent way for them to be able to delight in having some chocolate without needing to stress over the health issues that they would deal with from consuming commercially created chocolate.

Individuals that have serious allergies to things that are typically discovered in commercially made chocolate, like nuts, need to be exceptionally cautious about the types and brand names of commercially made chocolate that they consume and numerous people choose to create homemade chocolate so that they can be sure it's without any nuts or nut products.

This is a substantial issue for individuals that have diabetes due to the fact that chocolate can wreak havoc with a diabetic's blood glucose levels. Numerous physicians suggest that individuals who struggle with Diabetes quit chocolate completely or only consume sugar-free chocolate. Considering that it could be difficult to locate sugar free chocolate that is delicious and not pricey, making homemade sugar free chocolate a fantastic option for diabetics. If you have a diabetic member of the family, you can make that individual feel more at home at parties or on holidays by creating special homemade sugar-free chocolate that they can enjoy.

Another reason why you ought to give homemade chocolate making a shot is since it's enjoyable. If you take pleasure in cooking, then you are going to most likely truly take pleasure in the imaginative procedure of choosing what kind of chocolates to make, the experience of, in fact, making the chocolate, and after that naturally comes the fun of enjoying the chocolate. Creating homemade chocolate is a terrific rainy day activity that you may do with the kids to keep them occupied, and the chocolates that you make are fantastic presents and party favors for holidays, birthdays, and other events.

Making homemade chocolate can additionally be a lot more economical than purchasing commercially created chocolates, particularly around holidays such as Christmas or Valentine's Day. If you wish to have some excellent presents that individuals are going to truly enjoy without spending a fortune then you can create homemade chocolate presents for individuals that are special and customized and do not cost that much to create. The majority of people enjoy getting homemade presents, and nearly everybody likes chocolate, so offering the present of homemade chocolate is sure to be a hit.

Chapter 2—How Chocolate is Usually Made

Making chocolate using the conventional method could be done at home, although it's a long and involved procedure. If you wish to pursue making homemade chocolate as a pastime and it is necessary that you create all of your chocolate from the ground up, you may do that, however, you'll require some specialized tools and a great deal of time on your hands. Some individuals actually do delight in making chocolate from the ground up, so you ought to give conventional chocolate making a shot to see if it's a pastime that you have an interest in pursuing. Utilizing a conventional procedure to create the chocolate at home consists of numerous steps:

1. Selecting the beans. Chocolate is created from cacao beans, so when you initially start making chocolate the conventional way, you have to start with some top-quality cacao beans. There are providers on the Internet that offer various ranges of cacao beans in various price ranges, so if you are trying to find whole cacao beans, it isn't too difficult to discover them.

2. Roasting the beans. Cacao beans have to be roasted much like coffee beans. You could roast them at home on a cookie sheet in the oven by watching them thoroughly, or you can purchase a specialized cacao bean roaster for at-home usage if you're going to pursue standard candy making as a pastime. The beans are generally roasted for as little as 5 minutes or as long as 35 minutes depending upon the kind of bean and the taste that you wish to get.

3. Getting the chocolate out. After the beans are roasted, you want to crack open the external shell of the bean to make the chocolate that is inside out. There are numerous methods to do this in your home. You could lay the beans in a single sheet on a baking sheet or on a counter and utilize a hammer to split the shells open, then utilize a blow dryer on a low setting in order to blow the bean hulls far from the chocolate or you can utilize a juicer to achieve the identical aim. This action could be really chaotic, so make certain that you have a mop and bucket and a great deal of clean-up products standing by.

4. Grinding and Refining the chocolate. Now you have to grind the chocolate down as fine as you can. If you do this in your home, lots of professional chocolate makers advise utilizing a top-quality juicer to grind the chocolate. After the chocolate has actually all been ground as carefully as possible, you want to include sugar, preservatives, milk or anything else that you're intending on including in the chocolate to improve the taste. As soon as all the things are combined with the other components, the chocolate is going to have to be agitated gradually yet continuously. This procedure might require up to 12 hours to get the chocolate to precisely the right consistency. Specialists suggest utilizing a stand mixer on a low setting to hone the chocolate.

5. Tempering the chocolate. As soon as the chocolate has actually been completely fine-tuned, it has to be tempered prior to utilizing it. Tempering chocolate in your home could be a really complex procedure; however, if you wish to cheat a little and accelerate the process, you can utilize a microwave to temper your homemade chocolate. When the chocolate is tempered and is smooth, tough and glossy, it's prepared to be utilized or consumed.

Chapter 3-- Making Terrific Homemade Chocolate Easily

Does the procedure of creating chocolate in a standard method look like a great deal of effort that you do not truly wish to do? Some individuals enjoy the prolonged procedure of creating chocolate in a standard fashion; however, some individuals desire a quicker, simpler method to get homemade chocolate. For those individuals, choosing what to utilize to taste the chocolate and utilizing distinct molds is an enjoyable part of creating homemade chocolate.

To make it simpler to get to the enjoyable part of homemade chocolate making, you can bypass the conventional chocolate-making procedure and utilize special chocolate chips and wafers that are created for candy making. These chips and wafers are fantastic since you can melt them down in a double boiler and even in a microwave, and after that, you have an excellent smooth chocolate base to work from, and you can get imaginative choosing what to include in the chocolate to make it distinctively yours.

When you utilize these chips, wafers, and bricks of chocolate to create your own chocolate, you'll be astonished at how innovative you can be. For lots of people, the standard method of creating chocolate is far too tough and lengthy. Many people simply wish to have the ability to comprise some cool homemade deals within their kitchen area, they do not wish to do a great deal of research or look for special components or buy a great deal of expensive tools to simply create some chocolate at home.

If you are among those individuals that wishes to get right to the enjoyable part of making chocolate in your home, blending the chocolates and developing brand-new chocolate recipes, then you ought to absolutely purchase some chocolate base from a candy supply store or a craft shop and begin to make your own candy utilizing those melt and pour chocolates.

Utilizing melt and pour chocolate is additionally an excellent method to experiment with various chocolate tastes. You could get some extremely unique chocolate bases that have plenty of unique spices that would cost a fortune if you wished to purchase them separately. You can additionally get sugar free and low-fat chocolate bases that remove the requirement for you to purchase costly components or gauge components to create chocolate that is sugar free or low fat.

If you wish to have a great deal of enjoyment creating homemade chocolate, spare some cash, and make terrific presents that all your buddies are going to like, then making chocolate utilizing some fantastic melt and pour chocolate bases is going to be ideal for you.

Search in your neighborhood craft shop to see if they have candy-creating supplies or look online to discover a candy supply shop that offers a broad selection of various chocolates that you can utilize to create homemade chocolate.

Chapter 4-- Finest Kinds Of Chocolate to Utilize in Homemade Chocolate

When it concerns creating your own homemade chocolate, there are a great deal of various chocolates that you can utilize depending upon your tastes and who you are creating the chocolate for. For instance, dark chocolate has no milk items in it, so if you are creating chocolate for somebody that is a vegan or somebody that is lactose-intolerant, you ought to utilize a dark chocolate base since it does not include any milk. Here is a fast summary of the most typical kinds of chocolate that you can utilize to create your own homemade chocolate:

Unsweetened chocolate-- You most likely have some experience with unsweetened chocolate. Unsweetened chocolate is frequently utilized in baking to include a rich chocolate taste to food. You could unsweeten chocolate as a foundation to create sugar-free chocolate and utilize something aside from sugar to offer the chocolate a sweeter taste. Lots of people that are diabetic or are monitoring their sugar consumption are going to utilize unsweetened chocolate and a sugar alternative to create their own homemade chocolate.

Dark chocolate-- As formerly specified, dark chocolate has no milk in it, so it's fantastic to utilize it as a base for individuals that can't or don't want to consume milk or milk items. Some individuals additionally delight in the dark, somewhat bitter taste of dark chocolate.

Bittersweet chocolate-- This chocolate is a little sweeter than unsweetened chocolate that has no sugar in it in any way; however, it does have a bit of sugar in it. If you wish to create chocolate that has a lot less sugar than other kinds of chocolate, yet you do not wish to utilize a retail sugar replacement, you can utilize bittersweet chocolate as a foundation for your homemade chocolates.

Semi-sweet chocolate-- Semi-sweet chocolate is somewhat sweeter than bittersweet chocolate and has a somewhat greater sugar material, yet it still has a lower sugar material than many chocolates. Semi-sweet is among the most popular kinds of chocolates utilized in sweet making and is likewise typically utilized in creating chocolate chip cookies.

Milk chocolate-- Milk chocolate is abundant chocolate, which contains high amounts of sugar and at least 12% milk or milk solids. The majority of milk chocolate is created with condensed or vaporized milk. Milk chocolate is extremely sweet and has a really low cocoa material, so it does not have the bitter or have an extreme taste that other chocolates have.

White Chocolate-- White chocolate is actually not chocolate, it's a mixture made from cocoa butter, sugar, and milk that is frequently flavored with vanilla or other tastes. It's referred to as chocolate since it includes cocoa butter; however, there is no real cocoa in it.

You can constantly experiment with various tastes by blending and matching various kinds of chocolate too. For instance, a touch of milk chocolate may provide your semi-sweet homemade chocolate with a bit of richness that is going to boost the taste. Experiment with the various sorts of chocolate up until you discover a mix that truly tastes excellent and turn that into your "signature" chocolate base.

Chapter 5-- Tools for Creating Homemade Chocolate

Some books and publications about making candy are going to state that you have to have a great deal of special tools so as to create chocolate in your home; however, that's not always correct. There are truly just 5 tools that you need to have in order to make excellent chocolate at home, and you most likely currently have at least a few of them in your kitchen area. They are:

1. Candy thermometer-- Some chocolate candy does have to be warmed to a particular temperature level so as to be safe to consume, and some kinds of chocolate have to be warmed to a particular temperature level so as to be liquid enough to pour and set appropriately in a mold, so it's a great idea to have at least one candy thermometer ready.

2. Blending bowls-- You are going to go through blending bowls like crazy when you are creating chocolate, particularly if you are blending other components into a chocolate base. To conserve cash

on blending bowls, go to your neighborhood Goodwill or Salvation Army shop. Charity stores like that generally have kitchen and housewares parts where you can discover fantastic deals on glass and stainless-steel blending bowls. You can additionally try to find blending bowls at garage sales.

3. Pots and pans -If you are utilizing a pre-made chocolate base, you can warm that base in a microwave up until it's liquid enough to deal with. However, you are going to require saucepans to mix in other components and bring the chocolate to the appropriate temperature level. Much like blending bowls, you can typically discover mismatched pots and pans at charity shops and garage sales. You can additionally utilize 2 pans to create your own double boiler when a chocolate recipe requires utilizing a double boiler.

4. Molds-- When you have your chocolate mixed simply the way you desire it and have actually included any extras that you wish to include into the chocolate, you're going to require something to pour that chocolate into to ensure that you can create chocolate sweets. It's constantly a great idea to have

a wide array of chocolate molds that are tidy and all set to go.

5. Candy Coloring-- If you wish to truly embellish your handmade chocolates and create fun shapes and colors, you are going to have to utilize special sweet coloring. Regular food coloring is not going to color the chocolate. To get the colors to display on the chocolate, it's important to have unique food coloring that is created candy and chocolate. You can discover candy coloring at any sort of craft supply shop or candy supply shop.

These are only a handful of the materials that you may require to create chocolate; however, if you have these materials constantly on hand, then you should not have any difficulty making scrumptious homemade chocolates at any moment. If you are going to make a unique kind of chocolate or you wish to utilize a unique recipe, then you may require customized tools. However, in general, you can get by simply utilizing these tools and what you currently have in your kitchen area.

Chapter 6—How to Make Sugar Free Chocolate

In case you or a loved one is Diabetic or is on a diet plan where they can't withstand sugar, creating your own sugar-free chocolate is a terrific manner in which you or they can take pleasure in a sweet delight without sugar. If you are creating desserts for a celebration or supper and have buddies or family attending, it would be a thoughtful gesture to have some sugar-free chocolates on the menu that individuals who can't have sugar or are monitoring their sugar consumption might still have a good time.

There are numerous manners in which you can create your own sugar-free chocolate. In case you are skillful in the kitchen area and feel comfy creating your own chocolate, you can utilize a base chocolate such as unsweetened chocolate that has no sugar in it; however, you'll need to include something in the chocolate to sweeten it. In case you can utilize a sugar alternative that has the identical consistency that sugar has, that is most likely the very best path; however, you can additionally include things such as fruit juice to the unsweetened chocolate to make it sweeter.

When you are mixing unsweetened chocolate with a sugar alternative, you ought to constantly blend the two components when they are dry, or otherwise, they will not mix appropriately, and they are going to separate when they are wet. In case you are utilizing fruit juice to sweeten the unsweetened chocolate, pour in extremely tiny amounts and make certain that you include a thickener to the chocolate to maintain the chocolate at the ideal consistency.

In case you do not feel comfy attempting to take an unsweetened chocolate base and attempting to sweeten it on your own, you can purchase sugar-free or diabetic-friendly chocolate in blocks or in chips from candy supply shops, and after that, utilize that as a base for your chocolate treats. Many candy supply stores have a variety of sugar-free chocolates consisting of dark chocolate and milk chocolate that is all created with a sugar alternative so that it's harmless for anybody that can't eat.

When you have an unsweetened or sugar-free chocolate foundation, you are able to make chocolate candy the identical way that you would with routine chocolate by pouring it into molds and allowing the candy to harden. However, in case you wish to make an elegant chocolate dessert such as s chocolate dipping sauce for fresh fruit, chocolate mousse, or perhaps sugar-free hot chocolate, you can still utilize the sugar-free chocolate as a base, and after that, you can try various recipes utilizing the sugar-free chocolate as a component.

You can even create sugar-free chocolate chip cookies by slicing up little chips of the sugar-free chocolate base and including them in some sugar-free cookie dough, although you are going to need to be aware of what temperature level you bake the cookies at or the chocolate is going to melt.

If you are intending on making holiday delights or chocolates as presents for your kid's teachers, buddies, and next-door neighbors, or anybody that you do not know all that good, it's constantly an excellent idea to add at least a couple of sugar-free chocolates in the present bundle since you never ever know if somebody can have chocolate that has regular sugar in it or not. Individuals that can't have sugar are going to discover it really considerate that you included some sugar-free chocolates.

Chapter 7—How to Make Low Fat Chocolate

If you are on a diet plan or if somebody in your home is attempting to drop weight, then you may wish to attempt creating some low-fat chocolate that you can keep around your home or offer to your buddies as presents. Homemade low-fat chocolates are incredibly popular as desserts for sleepover celebrations or as party favors at teenage birthday favors. It's additionally great to have some low-fat chocolates around when you wish to have the ability to delight in some chocolate without needing to stress over just how much fat you're consuming.

One method to create low-fat chocolates at home is to search for some pre-made low-fat chocolate bricks or chips that you can melt down and utilize to make your own sweets. However, if you can't discover low-fat chocolate that is pre-made or you do not wish to invest a great deal of cash on an expensive pre-made chocolate base, you can quickly make your own low-fat variation of standard chocolate that you can utilize to create brownies, cookies, or candy. A low-fat chocolate dipping sauce for fresh fruit makes a terrific low fat and low-calorie dessert that is not going to make you feel like you're losing out on a delight.

Utilize these pointers to create your own low-fat chocolate:

- Establish a taste for dark chocolate. Given that dark chocolate has no milk items in it, dark chocolate hast the smallest fat material of the various types of chocolate.

- Replace semi-sweet or bittersweet chocolate for milk chocolate. The less cocoa butter and milk that the chocolate has, the lower the fat material is going to be.

- Do not include additions to your chocolate. In case you need to include something to the chocolate, go with some sliced nuts that are great for your heart or raisins that are healthier and lower in fat.

- Utilize a chocolate covering rather than chocolate. In case you are craving a sweet dessert, yet you truly wish to keep your fat consumption low, create a low-fat chocolate dipping sauce from some semi-sweet or dark chocolate, and after that, simply gently coat some fresh fruit, a granola bar, or some other low-fat, healthy treat with the chocolate. By doing this, you'll still get a chocolate fix; however, you will not be consuming a great deal of fat to obtain it.

- Make some low-fat hot chocolate rather than candy. Make some low-fat hot chocolate utilizing dark chocolate and take pleasure in a warm cup of hot chocolate rather than creating brownies or another kind of high-fat dessert.

- These are simply some basic manners in which you can still have chocolate treats without fretting about destroying your diet plan or overdoing it on your fat consumption. In case you have kids and you're worried by just how much fat your kids consume, simply using some low-fat chocolate as opposed to regular chocolate in cookies, brownies, and chocolate milk can make a huge distinction in just how much fat your kids are consuming daily.

Chapter 8—How to Make Your Chocolate Distinct

Among one of the most enjoyable aspects of creating your own homemade chocolate is that you can experiment with various components and create your own distinct chocolate recipes and chocolate delight. Putting your personal stamp on the chocolate that you create is going to make it more special when you provide the chocolate as presents to individuals that you like. And in case sooner or later you wish to go further and really sell the homemade chocolate that you create, then having your own distinct chocolates is going to make it a great deal less troublesome to sell your chocolate.

However, the majority of people that create homemade chocolate utilize the identical fundamental kinds of chocolate and the identical base chocolate blends from sweet supply shops, so how can you create your own distinct chocolates without creating your chocolate completely from the ground up? Here are 5 simple manners in which you can produce scrumptious delights that reflect your own individual design:

1. Mix chocolate bases-- Even if a great deal of individuals that create homemade chocolate utilize the identical bases, that does not suggest that you can't create your base chocolate special. You can utilize the identical chocolate bases from sweet supply shops that other individuals utilize, however, simply mix them in a distinct manner to create your own signature taste. Blending dark chocolate and milk chocolate, or semisweet chocolate with white chocolate, or blending other tastes together to develop your own distinct base could be a fantastic method to make your homemade chocolates stand apart from the crowd.

2. Include things to your base chocolate-- There are a great deal of things that you can include in your chocolate base to make your chocolates tastier and more special. You can utilize toasted sesame seeds to offer crunch, or you can utilize peanut butter, seeds, nuts, fruits, and a great deal of other things to make chocolates that are distinct and tasty.

3. Create your own molds-- Think outside the box when it concerns the molds that you utilize. Rather than simply utilizing conventional sweet molds in standard shapes, utilize cake molds, soap molds, cookie cutters, and other tools to make exciting and special shapes for your chocolates. If you wish to create your own molds, you can discover books and the materials that you require to create your own plastic molds at most craft shops.

4. Utilize distinct packages-- How you pack your sweets can end up being a signature design for you that is going to set your chocolate apart from other chocolates and apart from retail candy too. Rather than utilizing standard boxes, try to find exciting and special methods to package your candy, like utilizing a hand-painted box or small cello bags.

5. Utilize decors-- Utilizing sweet coloring and other exciting decors on your chocolates can assist you in turning even the simplest homemade chocolate into an exciting reward. Make certain that you package the sweet effectively to ensure that the decors do not fall off.

Chapter 9-- Molds

Utilizing molds is a terrific method to make your chocolate exciting and intriguing. You can utilize standard molds that are simply in standard shapes such as squares or bars, or you can utilize exciting molds that remain in all various shapes and styles. If you wish to create lollipops or suckers, there are unique molds that you can utilize to make those.

There are a great deal of businesses that make unique sweet molds that are particularly created to be utilized with chocolate. These are typically discovered in holiday shapes such as Easter bunnies, chicks, and eggs, or in Christmas shapes such as Santa Claus, stars, and Christmas trees. There are sweet molds out there for each season, so you should not have any difficulty discovering a mold that is going to be best for your holiday event.

However, you're not restricted to simply utilizing sweet molds for your chocolate. You can utilize soap molds, cake molds, or other kinds of molds too. Provided that mold is created from heavy plastic, it ought to work just great. To create your candy slide out of the mold more quickly, spray the interior of the mold with a no-stick cooking spray. This way, you will not have a circumstance where half of your chocolate candy winds up stuck within the mold. If chocolate does get stuck within a mold turn, the mold over to ensure that the open side is facing down and run the mold beneath the warm water tap up until the chocolate loosens up and moves out.

To look after your molds ensures that you clean every one completely after you're finished with it. Molds could be cleaned with regular soap and water like dishes. Most are not dishwasher safe, so do not place them in the dishwashing machine unless the mold states that it's dishwasher safe.

The moment you pour the chocolate into the molds, it may take a number of hours or perhaps a number of days for the chocolate to solidify in the mold. Despite the fact that you may be lured to place the chocolate and the mold into the freezer so that it solidifies faster, you should not do that. It is going to make the chocolate harden too quickly, and it can harm the mold. You can place the chocolate-filled mold in the fridge too, which ought to assist the chocolate in strengthening in the mold faster.

Utilizing molds is a low-cost and simple method to create your homemade chocolate more exciting. Getting your candy out of a mold could be challenging, however, one manner in which you can make it simpler to get the chocolate out of the mold once it's tough is to drop the mold onto the counter prior to you setting it down to loosen up the chocolate within the mold. Running the mold beneath a bit of warm water is additionally a great way to get chocolate candy out of a mold.

You can discover candy and craft molds at any craft shop, and often at the supermarket too. Some craft shops bring thin plastic molds that are really inexpensive, however, these do not last long, so they're not actually a bargain. Devote a couple of dollars more and get molds created from high-density plastic that are really thick. They're actually worth the additional expense.

Chapter 10—How to Make a Better Homemade Chocolate

When it concerns making homemade chocolates, everybody has their own favored techniques that they utilize, and actually, the only method for learning the very best method to make homemade chocolate is to make some. However, here are some fast suggestions that you can utilize to create your homemade chocolate much better that have actually been collected throughout the years by specialist chocolate makers and home chocolate makers alike. These ideas can make your homemade chocolate productions even better:

- When you purchase chips or wafers of chocolate that you are going to liquefy as a chocolate foundation for your candy, do not take them out of the plastic bags that they arrive in. Microwave them up until they are liquefied or utilize a double boiler to liquefy them, and after that, simply cut a little hole in the corner of the bag and utilize the bag like a pastry bag for pouring the chocolate into molds.

- The moment you microwave chocolate to liquefy it, begin with simply 1 minute, and after that, keep microwaving it in 1-minute increments up until it's liquefied. Every microwave is distinct, and each kind of chocolate has its own melting point, so the time required to liquefy the chocolate is going to be different on each microwave. Liquefying the chocolate in one-minute increments implies that you are not going to burn the chocolate mistakenly.

- Do not freeze your chocolate mixtures. Freezing is going to begin to make the chocolate fall apart, and you'll lose the scrumptious taste of homemade chocolate. Rather than freezing the chocolate, store it in an airtight container at room temperature level.

- Dark chocolate that is effectively covered and kept is going to remain great for about a year, however, milk chocolate is going to remain great just for about 6 months. If it's been longer than 6 months, search for white areas on the chocolate. If the chocolate has white spots, referred to as bloom, it suggests that the chocolate is beginning to separate, and you ought to eat it right away or toss it out.

- To reduce calories and make your homemade chocolate last longer, take the homemade sweets or chocolate bars that you created and slice them into a lot of little pieces. Wrap the pieces and place them in the fridge. The moment you or the kids desire a cold, sweet treat on a hot summertime day get a piece of the cold homemade chocolate. It is going to have less calories and fat than ice cream or a complete candy bar and is going to taste yummy.

- In case you're truly in a jam, and you require some chocolate to be done with creating a batch of homemade chocolate, and you run out chocolate and you do not have the time to go to the candy supply shop or craft shop to get more, or in case the craft and hobby shops near you do not have candy creating chocolate, you can manage with some melted chocolate chips. It's not a fantastic option, however, it's an option when you require some urgent chocolate for a recipe.

- In case your chocolate does establish bloom, and you will not consume it immediately yet do not wish to toss it out, you can melt the chocolate down, include some brand-new components, put it in brand-new molds, and after that, cover it and put it away.

Chapter 11—How to Wrap Your Homemade Chocolate

You can have a great deal of fun wrapping your homemade chocolate delight for a unique occasion, to offer as a gift, or just as a reward for the family or your buddies. There are a great deal of various manners in which you can package your homemade chocolate, however, when you're choosing wrapping for your homemade chocolate something that you want to bear in mind is that the chocolate has to be in something that is airtight in case it won't be consumed instantly.

Due to the fact that the initial issue is constantly keeping the chocolate fresh, homemade chocolate typically comes covered in 2 wrappers, one that is airtight and one that is ornamental. You can select a conventional gold-colored sweet box with pillow sheet inserts that are just like other sweet boxes. These are normally really comparable to the boxes of sweets that are prominent as Valentine's Day and Christmas presents.

Or you can utilize little cello bags that seal shut with a hairdryer or other heat source. Cello craft bags are user-friendly and are extremely affordable. Frequently they can be found in various colors or prints, so they are fantastic for covering homemade chocolates as party favors or birthday celebration treats. Cello bags could be discovered at any craft supply or sweet supply shop, or in case you are going to be utilizing a great deal of cello bags, you can purchase them in bulk online and get terrific savings.

In case you are creating lollipops or suckers, then cello bags are the very best packaging to utilize due to the fact that the cello bag will not stay with the chocolate like cling wrap is going to. Place a cello bag over the top of the sucker, utilize a hairdryer to warm up the cello bag, and the bag is going to mold to the shape of the sweet without staying with it. Place a ribbon or a sticker label on the sucker, and you have a hygienic bundle that is going to keep the chocolate fresh and looking lovely.

The packaging that you utilize for your homemade chocolates is practically as essential as the chocolate itself due to the fact that the packaging is the finishing touch. Whatever kind of packaging you select for your homemade chocolate ought to be special and ought to show your character.

In case you are creating homemade chocolates for an occasion or a holiday, utilizing unique style packaging reliably creates an excellent impression. Although you may believe it's not needed to invest a great deal of time or cash on wrapping your chocolate, it's actually worth it to take that final step and develop an exciting package for your chocolate.

After all, you strove to create a tasty treat, and in order to keep that treat scrumptious and safe to consume, it's essential to place some type of packaging on it. So select some cool packaging and even something sweet and conventional, however, make certain that whatever packaging you choose reveals a little bit of your character to make your chocolate actually special.

Imaginative packaging for your homemade chocolate does not need to be pricey to be excellent; it simply has to be something that you created yourself with your own creative stamp.

Chapter 12-- Homemade Chocolate Christmas Ideas

Holidays are a fun time to amaze your friends and family with homemade chocolates, and creating homemade chocolate for Christmas is certain to make the holiday more joyful. In case you want to offer individual presents to your friends and family, or in case you are attempting to keep your holiday budget plan low, creating homemade chocolates is a good solution to having fantastic, affordable presents.

Here are several ideas that you can utilize to make your Christmas holiday more joyful with homemade chocolate.

- Homemade chocolates that are covered in plastic, and after that, set up in a lovely holiday tin create fantastic economical presents for teachers, ministers, postal carriers, newspaper carriers, delivery people, and managers.

- When you have to bring a dessert to a holiday celebration, and you desire your dessert to actually stick out, make several homemade chocolates and organize them on a holiday serving plate with a fresh fruit garnish.

- Utilize some of your homemade chocolate to create some rich holiday hot chocolate to take pleasure in on a cold winter season night.

- Do you require presents for a lot of folks, like all individuals in your workplace, or each of the 30 kids in your kid's class at school? Put a couple of homemade chocolates in a little candy box and have your kid embellish the exterior of the package with markers, glue, and paint, and you have a distinct present that does not cost a lot or require a great deal of time to create.

- Utilize your holiday cookie cutters to cut out some homemade chocolate fudge in holiday shapes.

- Create sugar-free and low-fat homemade chocolates rather than Christmas cookies to attempt and keep the number of holiday calories that you under control.

- Create some homemade chocolate bark or chocolate cherry bark and place it on a plate with some fresh fruit and utilize that as an edible focal point for your holiday table.

Chapter 13-- Homemade Chocolate Drinks for Holidays

Practically everybody likes hot chocolate, and throughout the winter season holidays, hot chocolate drinks are all over. Hot chocolate is a fantastic drink to have at celebrations where individuals may not wish to consume alcohol and where kids are going to be present. Homemade hot chocolate blends additionally create fantastic presents.

So this year, rather than investing a great deal of cash on elegant hot chocolate blends to offer as presents or to keep in the kitchen for friends and family, you ought to create your own distinct hot chocolate blends that you utilize to serve hot chocolate to guests or utilize as presents.

Homemade hot chocolate blends are simple to create. The initial thing that you require to create homemade hot chocolate is cocoa powder. You can purchase sweetened or unsweetened cocoa powder in the supermarket; it's typically in the aisle where the syrups and chocolate milk powders are held.

Then you require some powdered non-dairy creamer or powdered milk. Creamer is going to make your homemade hot chocolate really abundant, so most experts recommend that you utilize primarily powdered milk, however, include a bit of powdered creamer simply to include a little bit of richness to your hot chocolate mix. Utilize a flavored non-dairy creamer to boost the taste of the hot cocoa.

As soon as you have cocoa powder and milk or creamer base, you can utilize your creativity and cooking abilities to assemble some amazing hot cocoa mix delights.

Here are some exciting ideas that you can utilize to create your own delicious hot chocolate this holiday season:

- For individuals that are diabetic or can't get sugar, utilize unsweetened cocoa, and utilize a sugar replacement to sweeten the cocoa powder.

- Include spices and herbs to create Mexican hot chocolate or other kinds of hot and spicy hot chocolate.

- Include dried fruit and herbs to provide your hot chocolate with a jolt.

- Include tiny marshmallows to create a hot chocolate mix everybody is going to like.

- Mix various kinds of cocoa powder to get various tastes.

- To create a low-fat hot chocolate mix, utilize dark cocoa powder and low-fat creamer and milk.

- To make a really individual present on a budget plan, make up numerous sorts of hot chocolate blends and wrap them in plastic bags that are inside lovely envelopes and load them in a basket with 2 mugs and some homemade cookies or chocolates.

As you're packaging your hot chocolate, it's a great idea to note all the components on the plan in the event somebody that you are offering the hot chocolate to is allergic to one of the components.

Chapter 14-- Homemade Chocolate Easter Ideas

Every chocolate enthusiast gets thrilled around Easter due to the fact that no Easter event would be complete without a great deal of chocolate. You can make the Easter holiday a lot more special and spare a great deal of cash on Easter baskets if you create your own homemade chocolate delights for Easter.

Because almost everybody overdoes it and consumes excessive chocolate throughout the Easter holiday, it's a great idea to create a low-calorie, low-fat, or sugar-free chocolate throughout Easter. That way, you can consume the very same quantity of candy, however, you'll be consuming less calories and less fat, and the same goes for your children.

Here are some suggestions that you can utilize to create your own homemade chocolates for Easter:

- Place your own twist on timeless chocolate bunnies by utilizing unique chocolates or an uncommon chocolate base like chocolate combined with spices or fruit to create chocolate bunnies.

- Create edible homemade chocolate baskets rather than chocolate bunnies, then organize other holiday delights within the basket. To create a chocolate Easter basket, melt some base chocolate in a plastic bag and blow up a little balloon. Place the balloon within the bag of melted chocolate up until the bottom half of the balloon is heavily covered with chocolate, and after that, instantly move the balloon to the fridge.

- Once the chocolate solidifies, pop the balloon and draw the balloon out, and you'll have a strong chocolate Easter basket that you can utilize for your children or as a holiday table focal point. You can even utilize white chocolate as a base and color it with food coloring to create your chocolate baskets in various colors. Beware though! The chocolate is going to melt if left out in the warm weather condition.

- In case you wish to minimize the quantity of sugar that your children are going to be consuming throughout the Easter holiday, create a chocolate dipping sauce, and after that, slice fruit into Easter shapes and dip the fruit into the chocolate. When the chocolate solidifies, your children are going to have a sweet holiday delight with a whole lot less sugar and calories.

- Rather than embellishing hard-boiled eggs in beautiful colors, create some dark chocolate eggs and utilize sweet coloring to paint the chocolate eggs the manner in which you would paint standard hard-boiled eggs.

- The majority of Easter sweets are created from milk chocolate, so keep away from utilizing milk chocolate in your homemade Easter sweet bases and utilize something more unique to make sure your homemade chocolate stands apart more.

Chapter 15-- Homemade Chocolate Ideas for Other Holidays

You can create a great deal of excellent presents, party favors, and focal points for other holidays too. Here are some exciting methods for utilizing homemade chocolates for other holidays:

For Valentine's Day

Absolutely nothing states "I love you" such as some homemade chocolates on Valentine's Day. Given that the cost of sweets and flowers typically goes sky high around Valentine's Day, creating your own homemade chocolates for your partner could be a terrific method to spare cash and still give that special somebody a present that they'll love. When you require a special homemade valentine treat, you can:

- Create homemade chocolates utilizing some "naughty" chocolate molds for a bit of fun.

- Plan a sensual dessert by chopping up some fresh fruit and creating an amazing, hot chocolate dipping sauce.

- Create a dozen chocolate rose lollipops rather than offering a dozen roses.

- Utilize Valentine-themed cookie cutters to create unique chocolate bars and fudge pieces.

- Create homemade chocolates that your kid can bring to school and share with schoolmates rather than purchasing pricey valentines.

- Surprise your sweetheart with heart-shaped pancakes and homemade chocolate sauce for breakfast.

- Create some special hot chocolate blends as presents for family and friends.

- Blend an incredible chocolate sauce and serve it warm over some cold ice cream.

- Have an Anti-Valentine's Day party and create some dark chocolate broken heart sweets for your buddies that are solo.

- Create homemade chocolate present bags for everybody in the workplace.

- Utilize Valentine's Day molds to develop chocolate Cupids, and after that, embellish them with candy coloring. Offer one to everybody you meet on Valentine's Day.

- Make yourself a unique Valentine's Day chocolate reward and load some dark chocolate truffles with champagne and a bit rosewater.

- Create a box of homemade chocolates for your partner and top every one with a rose petal.

For Mother's Day

Mother's Day is one more holiday that you can make a lot more memorable by offering homemade chocolate. Remember when you were small, and your mommy enjoyed the gifts that you created with your own hands? Mommies constantly appreciate handmade gifts the most, so this year make her some tasty homemade chocolate treats. The only restriction to creating homemade chocolate presents is your creativity, however, here are some ideas to get you started:

- Utilize a soap mold of a mother and kid in a cameo to create some unique Mother's Day chocolates. Ensure that you utilize a chocolate base that is comprised of mommy's favorite kinds of chocolate.

- Make a present basket for mommy that has homemade chocolates, special hot chocolate blends, brand-new mugs, and a relaxing CD to play when she wants to unwind.

- Make vouchers that guarantee your mother a homemade chocolate treat on a monthly basis, together with a visit from you.

- Take a seat and share a cup of tea and some homemade chocolate with your mommy.

- Create a sauce of mommy's preferred chocolate and sprinkle it over some buttered popcorn to make chocolate popcorn balls. Mommy is going to enjoy having a crispy, sweet treat to delight in when she's enjoying TV.

- Start Mother's Day off with a memorable breakfast of chocolate-covered fruit.

- In case you have kids, creating homemade chocolate is a wonderful method for the kids to make something to offer to their mom, however, constantly monitor them when they're around the hot liquid chocolate.

- Have your kids adorn present boxes with shine and crayons and load the boxes with homemade chocolates.

- Have each kid create a handprint in chocolate for mommy.

- Provide your mommy with the very best present you can provide her, the present of your time. Spend the afternoon in the kitchen area with your mommy creating homemade chocolate with each other and eating all that you create.

Handcrafted presents mean more to moms than perhaps anybody else, and creating some homemade chocolate to provide to your mommy is a present that she'll remember so this year, rather than purchasing her another bathrobe or taking her to an elegant brunch that is crowded and overpriced, simply make her some homemade chocolate and see her face illuminating.

Chapter 16-- Homemade Chocolate Birthdays Ideas

Birthday celebrations and homemade chocolate go together. There are a great deal of manners in which you can utilize homemade chocolate at birthday celebrations as an economical, simple-to-create party favor. Homemade chocolate is constantly a success; however, homemade chocolate is particularly welcome at children's birthday celebrations. Here are some exciting manners in which you can utilize homemade chocolate to perk up birthday celebrations.

- Create homemade chocolate lollipops for your child's birthday celebration. Lollipops and chocolate suckers are excellent party favors due to the fact that they could be separately covered, and they are simple to carry around. Even if your kid's birthday celebration is elsewhere like a restaurant or park or museum, you can quickly give out homemade chocolate suckers as celebration favors.

- Create sugar-free homemade chocolates in shapes that suit the style of the celebration. Get a bulk order, or little Chinese food take out boxes, the small white boxes with wire handles to place the chocolates in. You can obtain them in bulk online. Provide crayons, stickers, shine, glue, and other things, and let the children embellish their own favor box, and then fill the boxes with homemade sugar-free chocolate as the children are leaving. The other moms and dads are going to value that the sweets are sugar-free, and the children are going to have a sweet reward which they can take home.

- Create chocolate boxes for the children to place their other party favors into and take home. Chocolate boxes are constantly a hit at birthday celebrations. You can create chocolate boxes for adult birthday celebrations too, and place grownup celebration favors in them. Homemade chocolate boxes are constantly a preferred party favor.

- In case the children are old enough, organize one celebration activity where they can create their own chocolate. You can liquefy the chocolate in the microwave for them, but after that allow them to include their own items into the chocolate such as nuts, sweets, fruit and so forth and allow them to pick a mold, pour their chocolate mixture in it and by the time the celebration is over the chocolate ought to be tough and prepared to take home.

- For adult celebrations, establish a chocolate fountain streaming with some scrumptious homemade chocolate sauce and establish a fruit bar loaded with fresh fruit for dipping. This offers individuals that are worried about their calorie consumption with a low-calorie dessert option to a birthday cake.

- Utilize homemade chocolates as the rewards for a few of the party games and let every winner pick their own present bag loaded with tasty chocolates.

- At adult celebrations, offer a mug with an embellished package of the unique hot chocolate blend inside and print the recipe on the envelope so your visitors can create it at home.

It's practically a necessity that you serve something chocolatey at birthday celebrations. In case you are the type of individual that does not truly care about chocolate, then you can serve some homemade chocolate to your visitors to ensure that they are going to have some chocolate.

Chapter 17-- Homemade Chocolate Ideas for Weddings and Wedding Showers

You may not have actually thought of utilizing homemade chocolates as wedding or wedding shower favors; however, homemade chocolates are ideal for weddings and wedding showers. Homemade chocolate wedding favors are additionally a fantastic method for the groom and bride to spare some cash due to the fact that homemade wedding favors are going to cost a lot less than retail ones.

At a wedding, you provide the favors to your family and friends to thank them for coming to rejoice at the wedding with you. Considering that homemade chocolates are an extremely special and private present, they are the ideal "thank you" for family and friends. There are numerous manners in which you can include homemade chocolates into your wedding; however, here are simply a few of the most prominent manners in which individuals utilize homemade chocolates as wedding favors:

- Get some plastic champagne glasses and load them with separately covered homemade chocolates. Put a square of tulle over the top and connect the tulle down with a ribbon to ensure that the chocolates do not fall out. Put one at each invitee's seat.

- Chocolate boxes created in the form of a heart with the groom and bride's names and the date sculpted into them are sophisticated party favors that are a success with attendees. If you wish to make it more personal, sculpt each person's name into a chocolate box, simply make certain that you offer the appropriate box to the appropriate visitor!

- Bottles of chocolate dipping sauce branded with the groom and bride's name and the dates and a cute name are exciting wedding event favors.

- Offer your attendees packages of special hot chocolate and 2 mugs in a basket with a book of love poems and rules that claim that they have to sit and read the book jointly over a cup of extraordinary homemade hot chocolate.

- In the child's area, establish a station where children can create their own chocolate to keep them occupied. Simply make certain that they are monitored and that aprons are on-call.

- Have a chocolate fountain streaming with an exclusive "signature" chocolate taste and have lots of strawberries and other fresh fruit nearby for dipping.

- A terrific wedding event favor is wrapping a couple of homemade chocolates with a little, handwritten recipe book filled with excellent recipes for homemade chocolates.

Homemade Chocolate Ideas for Wedding Showers

Homemade chocolates are the best celebration favors for wedding showers. Many ladies like chocolate and love handmade things, so offering your family and friends some unique chocolates created just for them as a method of stating "thank you" to them for arriving to rejoice in your upcoming marriage is a charming method to let them understand you value them. Here are some exciting ideas that you can utilize to create handmade chocolate wedding shower favors for your family and friends:

- In case you have a "grown-up" wedding shower, then some homemade chocolates in adult shapes are a great deal of fun and a fantastic conversation piece.

- Among the most prominent wedding shower favors is a little box of homemade truffles or other elegant chocolates connected with a bow. Generally, the box and ribbon remain in the bride-to-be's wedding colors. If you wish to make the favors additionally unique, take a minute to compose an individual message on every box.

- Chocolate boxes are additionally exciting for wedding showers, specifically when they are loaded with other little presents.

- Little chocolate bars inscribed with the bride-to-be's name or a charming stating and covered in customized packaging are affordable and charming wedding shower favors if you have a great deal of people going to the shower.

- Considering that there are a great deal of ladies that monitor their weight extremely thoroughly, a low-calorie chocolate dipping sauce with fresh fruit would be a good alternative dessert at a wedding shower for ladies that do not want cake or other high-calorie desserts.

- A handmade chocolate dipping sauce in a customized bottle makes a good wedding shower favor. Make certain that you have a couple of sugar-free bottles for anybody that has to have sugar-free chocolate.

- You can additionally serve a "cake" comprised completely of little boxes of private homemade chocolates and embellished with ribbons in the bride-to-be's colors. Set up the boxes on a cake plate to appear like a layer cake, and you'll have a stunning alternative to a high-calorie cake that is currently portioned out.

- In case you wish to celebrate your relationship with the family and friends who have actually participated in the shower, a good party favor is a unique mug that contains a packet of homemade hot chocolate blend and a voucher for one afternoon chat with you where you can share the hot chocolate.

- Do you require a unique wedding shower favor for your maid of honor? Load a present basket filled with homemade chocolates, chocolate-covered popcorn, 2 DVDs of films that you constantly enjoy together, and a comfortable blanket to ensure that the two of you can get together, enjoy films, and share some homemade chocolates prior to the wedding.

Chapter 18-- Homemade Chocolate Ideas for Other Celebrations

You do not require a holiday or a wedding or a birthday as a reason to create some homemade chocolate. Homemade chocolates are constantly a delight, and nearly any celebration or event is more enjoyable with some homemade chocolate.

Whether you are trying to find an activity to keep the children occupied on a rainy afternoon, or a task that you and your kid may do together, or something unique that you can create for a buddy on a minimal spending plan, investing a little time and a little money creating homemade chocolate can truly cheer up your day, or your another person's.

Here are some simple and economical manners in which you can utilize homemade chocolates to lighten up somebody's day:

- In case you have actually been extremely occupied recently and have not had a great deal of time left over to do things with your children, make a date to spend simply an hour in the evening creating homemade chocolates with them. The procedure of creating chocolate is simple and enjoyable, and it is going to offer you an opportunity to reconnect with your children.

- Create some homemade chocolates in heart shapes after your partner goes to sleep and leave a little box of homemade candy connected with a red ribbon on his/her pillow the following morning.

- Surprise a colleague that has actually been having a tough time adapting to something at work with a "pick me up" present box of homemade chocolates and some exclusive tea and a mug.

- Leave some exclusive homemade hot chocolate blends in the break room at work to ensure that everybody can delight in a good sweet delight in the afternoon.

- Send a little box of homemade chocolates in fun shapes to school with your children for their teachers as a little "thank you" present.

- When one of your buddies has a terrible breakup or has relationship issues, leave a present basket on her doorstep with a DVD of a film she loves, some homemade chocolates, some wine, and brand-new silk pajamas or a comfortable bathrobe and slippers.

- Put little, separately covered pieces of homemade chocolate in your kid's jacket pocket at arbitrary times.

- Whenever you leave a tip for the waiter at your favored dining establishment or the barista that creates your coffee, leave a couple of separately covered homemade chocolates too.

- Bring over some homemade hot chocolate and 2 mugs to a lonesome next-door neighbor, then take a seat and talk and share the hot chocolate.

Chapter 19-- Gourmet Homemade Chocolate

The majority of the time, when folks consider creating homemade chocolate, they think of somebody working in the kitchen area and creating some chocolate that is delicious, however not truly the type of high-end chocolate that you discover in a gourmet shop someplace. However, you can make gourmet chocolate in your home, and it does not need to cost a fortune to make.

If you have an extremely advanced palette and you truly delight in gourmet chocolate, however, you do not like paying $7 or more for a gourmet chocolate bar you can quickly create your own gourmet chocolate in your home.

The components make the chocolate. Any time you are baking or preparing, the quality of the components that you utilize actually makes a distinction. In case you bake cookies with butter rather than margarine, you can taste the distinction. In case you utilize genuine vanilla extract rather than replica vanilla, you are going to taste the distinction. The identical idea applies when you're creating gourmet chocolate in your home. Utilizing just top quality components is a necessity in case you wish to make the sort of chocolate that your family and friends are going to swear you purchased from a gourmet store.

In case you wish to create gourmet chocolate, yet you do not wish to go to the extreme of buying cacao beans, roasting them, grinding them, and the whole conventional sweet making procedure, you can purchase melt and pour style chocolate bases that are created from higher-end components that the majority of the melt and pour style chocolate, however, you are going to want to get those from a specialized sweet-shop, not from the neighborhood craft and hobby shop.

Online there are a number of stores that focus on offering high-end gourmet chocolate making products to homemade chocolate makers. An online search ought to turn up a couple of stores that you can purchase top quality melt and pour style chocolate from. Another component that is truly crucial when you're creating gourmet chocolate are the additions that you're adding to your chocolate.

The secret to conserving cash on your additions is hitting up your regional farmer's market or grocery co-op to get the very best natural components at good prices. You can purchase natural nuts, create your own peanut butter blends, get unique organic and high-end syrups and oils and fresh herbs and sugars such as lavender and rosehips to include in your gourmet chocolate.

When you're creating gourmet chocolate, you can additionally include various sorts of high-end alcohol to your chocolate to provide it with a terrific unique taste. For instance, you might combine a top-quality dark chocolate base with some raspberry-flavored vodka and a couple of dried raspberries to create an incredibly dark and sweet homemade chocolate. Or you might include some premium cognac to a gourmet chocolate dipping sauce that you would utilize to dip fruit into.

Creating gourmet chocolate may require more practice than creating routine homemade chocolate since the tastes in gourmet chocolate have to be extremely subtle, however, in case you like gourmet chocolate, you can discover how to create it in your home and have a great deal of fun creating your own gourmet chocolate tastes.

Chapter 20-- Selling Homemade Chocolate and Making Money

When you have actually found the joys of creating homemade chocolate, and you have caused your family and friends to put on weight with your constant chocolatey presents, you may find that you have a genuine enthusiasm for creating homemade chocolate. In case you are really enthusiastic about creating homemade chocolate, and you wish to attempt and bring in a little additional cash, you might attempt selling your homemade chocolate.

The initial thing that you want to do in case you wish to begin selling your homemade chocolate is to learn what the licensing criteria are in your state to have a business kitchen and you are going to want to either have your kitchen checked or lease a kitchen area that has actually been examined. When you have a certificate stating that your kitchen is authorized, you can begin creating homemade chocolate for sale.

As soon as you have the essential documents to begin selling homemade chocolate, you'll need to determine what your specific niche market is. Who are you attempting to sell homemade chocolates to? Are you going to create homemade chocolate wedding favors and other celebration favors, or are you going to concentrate on creating homemade chocolates for presents, or do you wish to do it all and simply make as many kinds of homemade chocolate as you are able to?

In some cases, individuals begin selling their homemade chocolates by selling them at craft fairs, church sales, and other locations where they are currently known to the majority of individuals that are going there. Getting friends and family to purchase your homemade chocolate could be a terrific method to begin a little side business selling your homemade chocolate.

In case you choose to begin selling your homemade chocolate, then it's a great idea to take a seat and draw up a standard business strategy and set some objectives for your business. Even if you simply wish to sell your homemade chocolate part-time on the side, it assists to have a business strategy and some idea of what your business costs are.

When you're prepared to begin taking orders, you can establish a site where individuals can purchase homemade chocolates from you. Ensure that you do some research into the various kinds of shipping solutions offered and just how much every one costs due to the fact that each freight provider is going to have their own set of guidelines about delivering.

If you do not wish to bother with the inconveniences of delivering food, you can additionally sell wholesale to local shops and pastry shops. If you are creating gourmet chocolate in your home, then regional gourmet shops or your local food co-op may be thinking about purchasing your locally created homemade chocolate wholesale to sell in their shops. Local shops are going to additionally, in some cases, accept consignment sales where you pay them a portion of what you make.

In case you truly enjoy creating homemade chocolate, and you have actually established a great deal of your own unique and distinct recipes, and you like developing brand-new recipes, then you may additionally wish to think of selling homemade chocolate recipe books or creating a blog site about your enthusiasm for homemade chocolate making.

Homemade chocolate making could be a fantastic pastime, and it can make you some additional money too, if you want to put the time and work into making your business grow.

Conclusion

Ideally, you have gotten a great deal of ideas and discovered a lot about creating chocolate at home, thanks to this book. Creating chocolate in your home is an enjoyable, amazing pastime that could be a terrific method of showing your family and friends just how much they mean to you. Absolutely nothing informs somebody you value them quite like offering them a homemade present, and an edible present at the same time.

Creating homemade chocolate can additionally spare you a great deal of cash when it comes to presents. Birthday presents, holiday presents, anniversary presents, and other presents can get rather expensive and if you have a great deal of family and friends, then you most likely usually need to purchase a costly present for somebody. Creating homemade chocolate could be a lot less costly than purchasing presents, and it offers you an opportunity to create something actually distinct.

Creating your own homemade chocolate can additionally be a means for you to get to spend more time with your children. Parents that work and are really occupied typically do not get to spend a great deal of quality time with their kids and creating some homemade chocolate together could be a good opportunity to get in touch with your kids and speak about how they are doing while you make a delicious delight that you can take pleasure in together.

If you like to cook and you like creating homemade chocolate, and you ultimately wish to open your own small business creating homemade chocolate, then being imaginative is going to be the key to your success. The ideas and suggestions in this book ought to assist you in getting started.

I hope that you enjoyed reading through this book and that you have found it useful. If you want to share your thoughts on this book, you can do so by leaving a review on the Amazon page. Have a great rest of the day.

Printed in Great Britain
by Amazon